Blastoff! Readers are carefully developed by literacy experts to build reading stamina and move students toward fluency by combining standards-based content with developmentally appropriate text.

 Level 1 provides the most support through repetition of high-frequency words, light text, predictable sentence patterns, and strong visual support.

 Level 2 offers early readers a bit more challenge through varied sentences, increased text load, and text-supportive special features.

 Level 3 advances early-fluent readers toward fluency through increased text load, less reliance on photos, advancing concepts, longer sentences, and more complex special features.

★ **Blastoff! Universe**

Reading Level

Grade K

Grades 1–3

Grade 4

This edition first published in 2024 by Bellwether Media, Inc.

No part of this publication may be reproduced in whole or in part without written permission of the publisher. For information regarding permission, write to Bellwether Media, Inc., Attention: Permissions Department, 6012 Blue Circle Drive, Minnetonka, MN 55343.

Library of Congress Cataloging-in-Publication Data

LC record for Cheetahs available at: https://lccn.loc.gov/2023046598

Text copyright © 2024 by Bellwether Media, Inc. BLASTOFF! READERS and associated logos are trademarks and/or registered trademarks of Bellwether Media, Inc.

Editor: Betsy Rathburn   Designer: Brittany McIntosh

Printed in the United States of America, North Mankato, MN.

Table of Contents

What Are Cheetahs?	4
Long and Lean	8
On the Run	12
Learning to Hunt	18
Glossary	22
To Learn More	23
Index	24

What Are Cheetahs?

Cheetahs are super speedy cats! They are the world's fastest land **mammals**. They can hit speeds of 70 miles (113 kilometers) per hour!

Cheetahs live in grasslands and **savannas**. They are often found on mountains, too.

Nearly all cheetahs live in Africa. A small number live in the Asian country of Iran.

Cheetah Range

range =

Cheetahs are **vulnerable**. Their **habitat** is getting smaller. This causes their numbers to drop.

Long and Lean

tear mark

Cheetahs have yellow or tan fur with black spots. Their faces have black stripes called tear marks.

Long legs help cheetahs run fast. Long tails help them balance as they run.

Identify a Cheetah

Adult cheetahs are up to 5 feet (1.5 meters) long. Their tails add over 2 feet (0.6 meters)!

Size Comparison

house cat

height at shoulder
around 10 inches
(25 centimeters)

length (without tail)
around 18 inches
(46 centimeters)

cheetah

height at shoulder
30 inches
(76 centimeters)

length (without tail)
up to 60 inches
(152 centimeters)

Cheetahs can weigh over 140 pounds (64 kilograms).

On the Run

Cheetahs have excellent eyesight. This helps them hunt. They quietly follow **prey**. Their spots help them stay hidden.

When they get close, they chase prey! They catch their meals with strong jaws.

Cheetahs are **carnivores**. Gazelles and impalas are favorite foods. They also hunt the young of bigger animals like warthogs and oryx.

Cheetahs even eat fast. They do not want others to steal their meal!

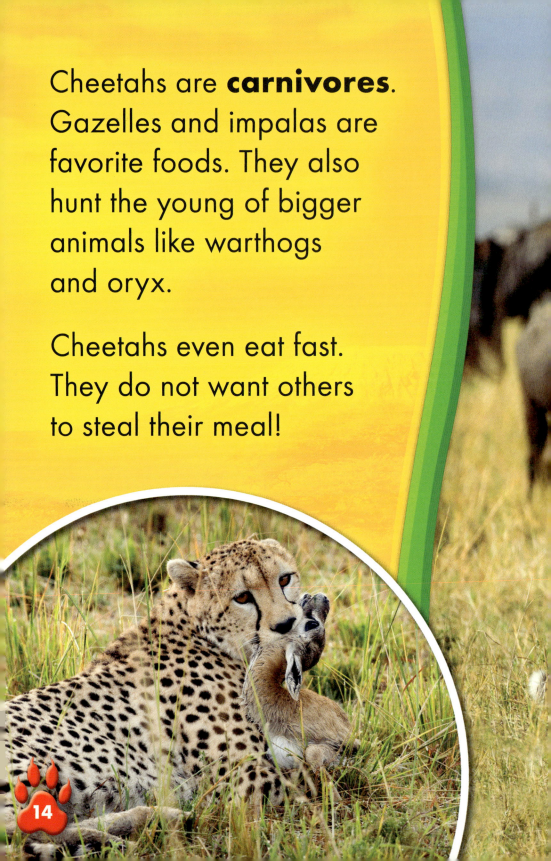

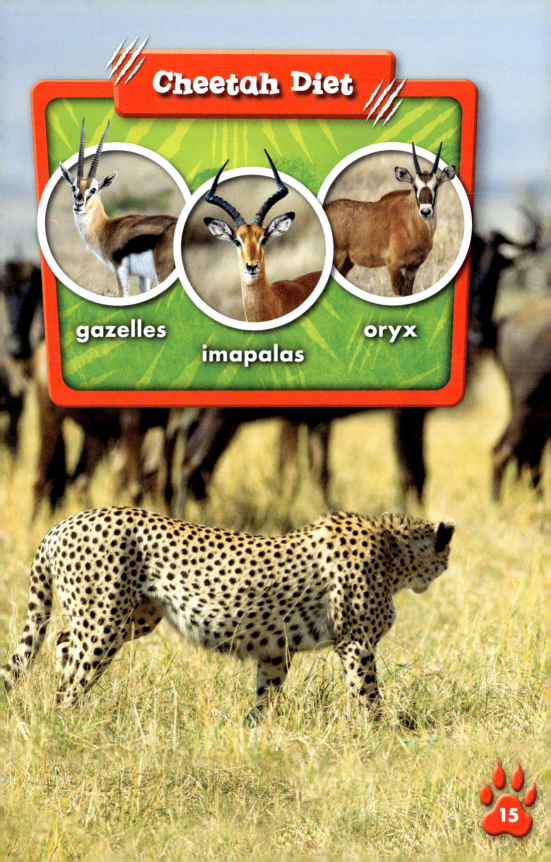

Adult male cheetahs live in groups called **coalitions**. These usually contain two or three brothers.

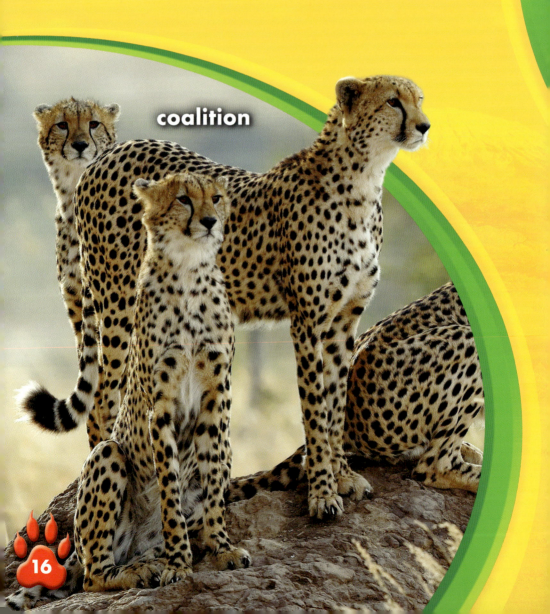

coalition

Adult female cheetahs often live alone. When they have cubs, they live with their babies.

Learning to Hunt

Females have babies during the wet season. There is more food at this time. Their **litters** usually have up to six cubs.

The cubs play and fight with each other. They practice **stalking**.

Baby Cheetahs

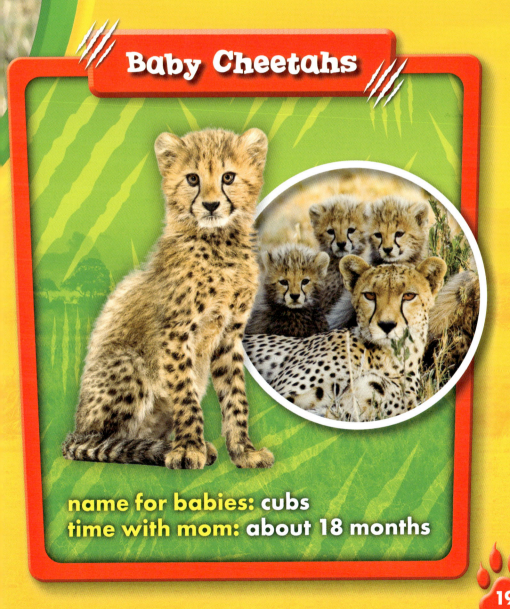

name for babies: cubs
time with mom: about 18 months

Cheetah moms teach their cubs to hunt.

Moms leave their cubs after about 18 months. The cubs stay with their brothers and sisters. Soon they are all grown up!

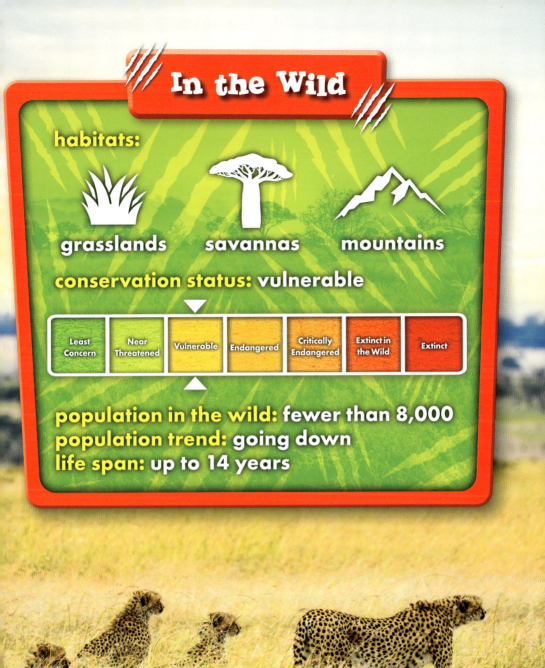

In the Wild

habitats:

grasslands   savannas   mountains

conservation status: vulnerable

| Least Concern | Near Threatened | Vulnerable | Endangered | Critically Endangered | Extinct in the Wild | Extinct |

population in the wild: fewer than 8,000
population trend: going down
life span: up to 14 years

Glossary

carnivores—animals that only eat meat

coalitions—groups of adult male cheetahs that live together

habitat—a land area with certain types of plants, animals, and weather

litters—groups of babies that are born at the same time

mammals—warm-blooded animals that have backbones and feed their young milk

prey—animals that are hunted by other animals for food

savannas—grasslands in warm areas that have few trees

stalking—hunting slowly and quietly

vulnerable—at risk of becoming endangered

To Learn More

AT THE LIBRARY

Geister-Jones, Sophie. *Cheetahs*. Mendota Heights, Minn.: Apex, 2022.

Grack, Rachel. *Cheetahs*. Minneapolis, Minn.: Bellwether Media, 2023.

Rustad, Martha E.H. *All About Baby Cheetahs*. North Mankato, Minn.: Pebble, 2022.

ON THE WEB

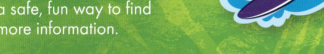

Factsurfer.com gives you a safe, fun way to find more information.

1. Go to www.factsurfer.com.

2. Enter "cheetahs" into the search box and click 🔍.

3. Select your book cover to see a list of related content.

Index

Africa, 6
Asia, 6
carnivores, 14
coalitions, 16
colors, 8
cubs, 17, 18, 19, 20
eyesight, 12
females, 17, 18, 20
food, 14, 15, 18
fur, 8
grasslands, 5
habitat, 7
hunt, 12, 20
identify, 9
in the wild, 21
Iran, 6
jaws, 13
legs, 9
litters, 18
males, 16
mammals, 4
mountains, 5

numbers, 7
prey, 12, 13, 14, 15
range, 6, 7
savannas, 5
size, 10, 11
size comparison, 11
speed, 4, 9, 14
spots, 8, 12
tails, 9, 10
tear marks, 8
vulnerable, 7
wet season, 18

The images in this book are reproduced through the courtesy of: Eric Isselee, front cover (cheetah), pp. 3, 9 (cheetah), 19 (cub), 23; Paul Hampton, front cover (background); Welshboy2020, p. 4; Michal Ninger, p. 5; Alamin-Khan, p. 6; Wayne Marinovich, p. 8; Chris Hill, p. 9 (inset); Stu Porter, pp. 10-11; Nynke van Holten, p. 11 (house cat); GoodFocused, p. 11 (cheetah); Freder, p. 12; Vladimir Turkenich, p. 13; Vaclav Sebek, p. 14; Stu Porter/ Alamy, pp. 14-15, 20; Gaston Piccinetti, p. 15 (impala); Volodymyr Burdiak, p. 15 (gazelle); liv_flu, p. 15 (oryx); Malyshev1974, p. 16; Matrishva Vyas, p. 17; Nature Picture Library/ Alamy, p. 18; GUDKOV ANDREY, p. 19 (inset); Jorge Sanchez Photos, pp. 20-21.